100 Second Best Poems

Poems Chosen by C. LEWIS HIND

"*She does not rank among beautiful women,
She has her moments for outshining them.*"

The Amazing Marriage. GEORGE MEREDITH.

LONDON: A. M. PHILPOT, LTD.
69 GREAT RUSSELL STREET, W.C.1
1925

First published Nov., 1925
Second impression, March, 1926

PRINTED IN GREAT BRITAIN

Dedicated to
All Second Best Poets

ACKNOWLEDGMENTS

TO Poets and Publishers, to Editors of Newspapers and Journals, to Correspondents who have sent him contributions the Compiler of this Anthology begs to tender his sincere thanks. He hopes to be forgiven if he has unwittingly infringed any copyright, or hurt any Poet by Publicity.

Special acknowledgments are made to the old *Westminster Gazette* (a nest of poets), the *Pall Mall Gazette* and the *Academy*. Also to the *Morning Post*, the *Observer*, the *Daily Chronicle*, the *London Mercury*, the *Poetry Review*, the *New York Evening Sun*, the *Touchstone* (U.S.A.), the *Outlook* (U.S.A.) and the *Sydney Bulletin*.

Also to the following publishers :—Messrs. Hodder & Stoughton, G. B. Putnam's Sons, Nisbet & Co., Elkin Matthews, and the Chairman of Hymns Ancient and Modern.

CONTENTS

X. THE ETERNAL HOPE.

XI. HYMNS.

EXPLANATION.

By C. LEWIS HIND.

I SHRINK from defining a Second Best Poem; but if the startled reader will continue to the end of this Explanation, he may guess what I mean by a Second Best Poem. If he be still in doubt there are 100 examples inviting him.

First let me draw attention to the extract from *The Amazing Marriage*, by George Meredith, on the title page— a happy find : "She does not rank among beautiful women. She has her moments for outshining them."

That saves me from recriminations by any poet who finds himself included in this collection. And the title of the book protects me from the reproaches of such among my poet friends who find themselves omitted. I may say to them, "My dear fellow," or "My dear woman, I couldn't include anything by You in a Second Best Collection."

The compilation of this Anthology began in a conversation, and, like Topsy, it "growed." It began by chance. For no one, in his senses, awakes on a spring morning and says suddenly to his breakfast tray, "I will make an Anthology of 100 Second Best Poems." Ah, perhaps the right way is to explain how the Anthology began.

* * * * *

The scene was a literary luncheon party at a London hotel. Having blunted the edge of appetite, I turned to my neighbour and opened conversation by inviting her to share what was uppermost in my mind—a way I have.

I said, "Have you seen to-day's *Times Literary Supplement*?" Of course I did not desire an answer: I wanted to enlarge upon something that I had seen in that excellent journal. So I continued, "In the correspondence columns there is a curious letter from a gentleman in Rotterdam, asking the Editor if he can give some information about a poem called *Child of my Love, Lean Hard*, which, he says, has been translated into Dutch, and is of some importance in connection with the biography of the late Dr. Kuyper, the famous Dutch statesman."

"Well?" said my fair (no, she is dark) neighbour.

"Why," I replied, "I can answer that question, and perhaps the Editor of the *Times Literary Supplement* cannot. I know *Child of my Love* by heart. It was given to me as a youngster, printed upon a card; and for months it hung above my bed. I dare say thousands of people have had a similar experience. *Child of my Love, Lean Hard*, is a first-class example of a Second Best Poem."

"What is a Second Best Poem?" asked my dark neighbour. Before I could reply she continued, with a smile, "I think I have a Second Best Poem in my bag. I was at a wedding yesterday, and they sang *O Perfect Love*. Here it is." She withdrew the hymn from her Vanity Bag, and as the others were now listening, I persuaded her to read it aloud, somewhat to the astonishment of the waiters. Infected by her charming boldness, I recited *Child of my Love, Lean Hard*; and another member of the party, an American, from Buffalo, followed with the last stanza of Dr. Carruth's *Each in His Own Tongue*:

> A picket frozen on duty,
> A mother starved for her brood,
> Socrates drinking the hemlock,
> And Jesus on the Rood,
> And millions who, humble and nameless,
> The straight, hard pathway trod—
> Some call it Consecration,
> And others call it God.

There was a brief silence, which I broke by saying, cheerfully, " If I were compiling an Anthology of 100 Second Best Poems, I should certainly include those three, and some from Longfellow, who is the supreme Second Best Poet, and *God and I in Space Alone*, and the *Canadian Boat Song*, and *Dickens in Camp*, by Bret Harte, and *The Stately Homes of England*, by Felicia Hemans."

" Second Best Poems," I continued, " are those that people cut out or copy out from newspapers and mazagines, and preserve, and read again and again, and hand around to their intimates. They are not usually included in Anthologies ; they are often of a devotional character ; they express longing, regret, gratitude and the joy of serenity ; they often have an ' uplift ' (I looked towards the American from Buffalo), and they depend rather on the heart cry in them than upon technical efficiency. They can also be lighthearted—even funny. Many of them are continually travelling round the world in newspapers. Editors ' lift ' them. Readers often recite them in the home circle. Why *I Have Lived And I Have Loved*, by L.S., that was published years ago in the *Sydney Bulletin*, is never at rest. And again and again have I seen quoted (author unknown) :

> God came to me as Truth, I knew Him not ;
> He came to me as Love, and my heart broke,
> And from its depths there came a cry,
> ' My Father, O my Father, speak to me,'
> And the great Father smiled.

And (author also unknown : very popular) :

> Oh, the gladness of her gladness when she's glad !
> And the sadness of her sadness when she's sad !
> But the gladness of her gladness,
> And the sadness of her sadness,
> Are as nothing to the badness of her badness
> When she's bad.

But if any of you want to know how far-flung is the public appreciation of Second Best Poems, you should consult the columns of the newspapers and journals, such as *The Sunday Times, John O'London's Weekly, Notes and Queries*, which regularly print literary enquiries and answers about poems that the public has loved and lost. Not long ago *The Sunday Times* received over one hundred answers, many correspondents copying out the entire poem, in reply to the question, 'Can you kindly inform me who wrote :

> By Nebo's lonely mountain
> On this side Jordan's wave,
> In a vale in the land of Moab
> There lies a lonely grave.'

Little did the late Mrs. Alexander think of the fame that was awaiting her noble Second Best Poem." *

And then—just as I was teaching myself something about my subject, a female Movie Star, in a radiant costume, sailed past our table and, having entirely lost the attention of my audience, I was obliged to cease talking.

When the Movie Star had sailed forward to a table decked with flowers and garlands, my dark neighbour leaned towards me, and whispered, "Will you compile for me an Anthology of 100 Second Best Poems ? "

I stared. I frowned. I laughed. I gave a gesture of animated resignation and said, "Oh, that's another matter. Do you really want me to exchange the dream for the business ? "

* * * * *

Here it is necessary, momentarily, to withdraw a curtain, and to allow the reader a glimpse into the mystery of the relation between a publisher and an author. For my dark neighbour is a publisher—A. M. Philpot, Limited, her real name being—no, I won't tell it ; but she deserves publicity for her pertinacity in urging me to compile the Anthology of 100 Second Best Poems. I wanted to

* See pape 160.

play with the idea ; she is a poetry enthusiast, and wished to convert it into something that would enable others to share our pleasure.

Weeks passed. The subject increasingly interested me. Desirous of learning something about the popularity of Second Class Poems, I wrote an article for *The Daily Chronicle*, and asked the readers of that journal to send me copies of their favourite Second Best Poems. The result was extraordinary. I was, to quote an unliterary friend, "fairly snowed up," with poems, and as many of my correspondents sent six and more, I had enough for half-a-dozen Anthologies. A tabulation of the offerings showed what a hold poetry of the " heart-to-heart " kind has upon people.

Child of my Love, Lean Hard, (see page 31) headed the list. Whittier was a good second with *At Last* (see page 153), and with :

> I know not where His islands lift their fronded palms in air,
> I only know I cannot drift beyond His Love and care.

Many correspondents sent in poems by—well, by "Best Poets"—some alive. I refrain from mentioning their names. One reader submitted Gray's *Elegy*. That was curious, because from her Anthology, *The Flower of the Mind*, Mrs. Meynell excluded Gray's *Elegy* for the reason that it is below the high-water mark of genius. To make her point she quotes this couplet from Gray :

> Full many a flower is born to blush unseen,
> And waste its sweetness on the desert air.

as against Shakespeare's :

> The summer flower is to the summer sweet,
> Though to itself it only live and die.

Could better examples of the difference between great Greatness and lesser Greatness be offered ?

* * * * *

The next adventure in my education as an Anthologist

was an invitation from the secretary of the Poetry Society, to give a Reading—" Anything you like "—at the Savoy Chapel. The subject I chose was "Some Second Best Poems," for those hundreds from *Daily Chronicle* readers offered ample material. But I did not read many of them from the Savoy pulpit. I argued that this Anthology must be My Anthology—containing poems that, for better or worse, have touched or moved me. All poetry-loving people, if they have the courage, could compile a personal Second Best Poems Anthology.

So I turned to my Note Books, that I had been thinking of subconsciously, and smiling over, ever since that luncheon party. These Note Books, now amounting to more than fifty, I have, through the years, filled from cover to cover. On the left-hand page I scrawl my brief Diary ; on the right page I cut out or copy out poems and prose passages from anywhere—usually by unknown people—that I wish to remember.

I conveyed piles of these old Note Books to the Savoy Chapel, and read aloud such Second Best Poems as I wished my audience to appreciate.

It was a strange experience. A storm was raging ; there was thunder and lightning : and there was I uncovering the predilections, in verse, of my lost youth, and of my mature years. One reporter, a nice fellow because he said nice things about the Reading, expressed surprise and pleasure at hearing fragments of the war songs—*Tipperary*, and *Oh Joy, Oh Boy*. I quoted them because the British Tommy and the American Doughboy chose, with unerring instinct, from the latest trivialities of Leicester Square and Broadway, the Second Best Songs that, incidentally, had an esoteric as well as an exoteric meaning—in *Tipperary* :

> It's a long, long way to Tipperary,
>   It's a long way to go ;
> It's a long, long way to Tipperary,
>   To the sweetest girl I know ;

> Good-bye, Piccadilly,
> Farewell, Leicester Square !
> *It's a long, long way to Tipperary,*
> *But my heart's right there !*

And in the American song :

> Where do we go from here, boys,
> Where do we go from here ?
> Slip a pill to Kaiser Bill and make him shed a tear ;
> And when we see the enemy, we'll shoot them in the rear—
> *Oh Joy, oh Boy, where do we go from here?*

Remember that the war had then been raging for a long time. Death threatened all. When the Americans went over the top at St. Mihiel, they sang, *Oh Joy, Oh Boy, where do we go from here?*

I refrain from quoting Fletcher of Salton. Let a modern—Oliver Wendell Holmes—speak, " I would rather risk, for future fame, upon one lyric than upon ten volumes."

I was asked to repeat this Reading at the Lyceum Club. The Dark Lady of the Luncheon Party was present, and at the conclusion she informed me, with a firm smile, that she had quite made up her mind to publish an Anthology of " 100 Second Best Poems " chosen by me.

" So the dream has really become a business," I said. " Well ! Well ! "

* * * * *

At once the difficulties started. As soon as I began to make the selection I decided—there was no other course—that I must not include Best Poets, even if they occasionally wrote Second Best Poems ; so Coleridge had to pass out—Coleridge with his beautiful and consolatory :

> Ere on my bed my limbs I lay,
> It hath not been my use to pray
> With moving lips or bended knees,
> But silently, by slow degrees,

17

My spirit I to love compose,
In humble trust mine eyelids close
With reverential resignation ;
No wish conceived, no thought exprest,
—Only a sense of supplication ;
A sense all o'er my soul imprest
That I am weak, yet not unblest,
Since in me, round me, everywhere,
Eternal strength and wisdom are.

Charles Lamb I could include : he is a Best Essayist, but a Second Best Poet.

But Walt Whitman had to go with his *At the Last, Tenderly*, and T. E. Brown, with his *A Garden is a Lovesome Thing, God Wot !* and his *O, Blackbird, what a Boy You Are !* T. E. Brown was a schoolmaster, but poetry was his real life.

On reflection, I excluded William Morris, with his :

From township to township, o'er down and by tillage
Fair, far have we wandered and long was the day ;
But now cometh eve at the end of the village,
Where over the grey wall the church riseth grey.

Lesser names, too, but real poets, Lionel Johnson, for example. Certain stanzas by him I love, such as his poem inspired by his memory of Walter Pater :

Gracious God keep him ; and God grant to me
By miracle to see
That unforgettably most gracious friend
In the never-ending end.

And his :

Do what thou wilt, thou shalt not so,
Dark Angel ! Triumph over me ;
Lonely unto the Lone I go ;
Divine to the Divinity.

And Dora Sigerson Shorter's :

The kine of my father, they are straying from their keeping,
The young goat's at mischief, but nothing can I do,
For all through the night I heard the Banshee keening,
Oh, youth of my loving, and is it well with you ?

Regretfully I had to omit that most touching little thing, an *Epitaph* by Walter de la Mare, which is underscored in one of my Note Books, and which I cannot call a Second Best Poem :

> Here lies, but seven years old, our little maid ;
> Once of the darkness—oh ! so sore afraid.
> Light of the World—remember that small fear
> And when nor moon nor stars do shine—draw near !

Neither could I include Sir Henry Newbolt's :

> There's a breathless hush in the Close to-night—
> Ten to make and the match to win—
> A bumping pitch and a blinding light,
> An hour to play and the last man in.
> And it's not for the sake of a ribboned coat,
> Or the selfish hope of a season's fame,
> But his Captain's hand on his shoulder smote—
> " Play up ! play up ! and play the game."

A friend said " Of course you will put in Kipling's *If* ? " I replied, " Of course I cannot. Kipling—is Kipling." Neither could I put in that other *If*, by Coleridge :

> If I had but two little wings
> And were a little feathered bird,
> To you I'd fly my dear.

Another friend pleaded for Wordsworth's *We are Seven*. The answer was in the negative. Wordsworth, although he wrote some Second Best Poetry, is among the Immortals. It comes to this : Usually, I omit those who have made their reputation by poetry, and who have virtually had no other aim in life than the making of poetry.

With George Eliot, Charles Lamb, Leigh Hunt, James Russell Lowell, John Hay, and R. D. Blackmore, I feel on safer ground. They were poets on occasions only. Longfellow, as I have already observed, is the supreme Second Best Poet. I have included four by him ; there might have been a dozen. How did I have the heart to leave out :

> And Deering's Woods are fresh and fair,
> And with joy that is almost pain
> My heart goes back to wander there,
> And among the dreams of the days that were,
> I find my lost youth again.
> And the strange and beautiful song,
> The groves are repeating it still ;
> A boy's will is the wind's will,
> And the thoughts of youth are long, long thoughts.

It will be noticed that many of my One Hundred Second Best Poems are from newspapers. Indeed, when I remember the past *Westminster Gazette,* and the *Pall Mall Gazette*, with their daily example of " Occ. Verse," and the present *Morning Post, Sunday Times, Observer and Daily Chronicle*, I feel that an alternative Anthology might be compiled, called Newspaper Poems. When an Editor is interested in poetry, he draws the best Second Best Poetry to him.

*   *   *   *   *

While preparing this collection I accumulated many couplets and quatrains, too slight for inclusion, yet such good examples of Second Best Poetry that I give myself the pleasure of quoting a few.

Let me begin with an enquiry addressed to the Editor of *The Spectator*, from a *Nonagenarian and Another*, for the author of the following couplet, and the poem from which it is taken :

> There shall come an end to the live long day,
> When thou shalt be weary but not with play.

Elsewhere a correspondent wishes to trace and rectify :

> Their good swords rust,
> Their bones are dust,
> Their souls are with the saints we trust.

A third seeks the author of the following, which R. L. Stevenson loved :

> When I was young and had no sense,
> I bought a fiddle for eighteen pence,
> And the only tune that I could play
> Was over the hills and far away,
>   So early in the morning,
>   Before the break of day.

Then there is *Einst, O Wunder*, from Matthisson's song, *Adelaide*, set to music by Beethoven. Stevenson refers to it in *The Ebb Tide*, and in one of his letters speaks of it as being "the most perfect love-song ever written— ideal words wedded to ideal music." But the world quotes only a line and a bit of it :

> Once, O Wonder ! once from the ashes of my heart
> Arose a blossom.

Another is this Southern example of the eternal lament :

> Oh, carry me back to Tennessee,
> There let me live and die,
> Among the fields of yellow, yellow corn—
> In the land that she loved, let me lie !

A great favourite is the couplet from a poem by Frederick Langbridge :

> Two men look out through the same bars ;
> One sees mud—and one sees stars.

The following, so often quoted, is from a poem by the Rev. G. A. Studdert-Kennedy (Woodbine Willie) :

> God gave his children memory,
> That in life's garden there might be
> June Roses in December.

This (author unknown) is remembered by many :

> True is the saying, that in common lives
> There dies a poet and the man survives.

In some he dies hard, and, before he dies,
Keeps in the half-extinguished spirit-eyes
Just sight enough to know he cannot see ;
And so the poet that still breathes in me
And strives his fitful essence to prolong,
Once to the joy departing made this song.

This, too, is remembered from *A Legend of Provence*, by
Adelaide Ann Proctor :

No star is ever lost we once have seen ;
We always may be what we might have been.

Also the epitaph found in many churchyards, in varying
forms :

Our life is but a winter's day,
Some only breakfast, then away :
Others to dinner stay, and are full fed ;
The oldest man but sups and goes to bed.
Large is his debt who lingers out the day,
Who goes the soonest has the least to pay.

And the lines by John Boyle O'Reilly, quoted by the
late John E. Redmond, in his last speech in the House of
Commons :

Gone, gone for ever is the fond belief,
The all too generous trust in the ideal ;
All my divinities have died of grief
And left me wedded to the rude and real.

And the chorus of Albert Chevalier's *My Old Dutch* :

We've been together now for forty years,
An' it don't seem a day too much,
There ain't a lady living in the land,
As I'd swop for my dear old Dutch.

And the song by Fred E. Weatherly which begins :

Three things in the world there be,
  Dear to my heart and eyes :
The broad green land, the mighty sea,
  And the eternal skies.

And Louisa Imogene Guiney's :

> A short life in the saddle, Lord,
> Not long life by the fire.

And—for these Second Best Snatches are as delightfully mixed up here as in the correspondence columns of newspapers—there are Edward Hazen Parker's lines, carved on President Garfield's tomb :

> Life's race well run,
> Life's work well done,
> Life's victory won,
> Now cometh rest.

And Longfellow's :

> Live I, so live I,
> To my Lord heartily,
> To my Prince faithfully,
> To my neighbour honestly,
> Die I, so die I.

And, in lighter vein, there is the *Newspaper Waif*, that Congressman Joseph G. Cannon, from Illinois, better known as Uncle Joe Cannon, was fond of quoting :

> I'm thankful that the sun and moon
> Are both hung up so high
> That no pretentious hand can stretch
> And pull them from the sky.
> If they were not, I have no doubt,
> But some reforming ass
> Would recommend to take them down
> And light the world with gas.

And certain wise quatrains—pleasant platitudes with a point—that trickle into newspapers and albums all over the English-speaking world, such as Charles Kingsley's :

> Do the work that's nearest,
> Though 'tis dull at whiles,
> Helping, when you meet them,
> Lame dogs over stiles.

And (author unknown) :

> 'Tis well to be merry and wise,
> 'Tis well to be honest and true ;
> 'Tis well to be off with the old love
> Before you are on with the new.

And (possibly by the Earl of Rochester) :

> It is a very good world to live in,
> To lend, or to spend, or to give in ;
> But to beg or to borrow, or to get a man's own,
> It is the very worst world that ever was known.

And Thomas Brown's (the idea, maybe, derived from Martial) :

> I do not love thee, Dr. Fell,
> The reason why I cannot tell ;
> But this I know, and know full well,
> I do not love thee, Dr. Fell.

And who, at times, has not tried to remember the Old Rhyme :

> Monday's child is fair of face,
> Tuesday's child is full of grace,
> Wednesday's child is full of woe,
> Thursday's child has far to go,
> Friday's child is loving and giving,
> Saturday's child works hard for its living,
> And a child that's born on the Sabbath day
> Is fair and wise and good and gay.

Finally, may I turn to the " In Memoriam " columns of *The Times* that contain so many touching fragments of poetry chosen by the bereaved. They confront us on the anniversaries of hard battles in the Great War.

The quotation oftenest used is from *For the Fallen*, by Laurence Binyon :

> They shall grow not old, as we that are left grow old ;
> Age shall not weary them, nor the years condemn—
> At the going down of the sun and in the morning
> We will remember them.

Another that appeals to many mourners is a line from Swinburne, but they rarely give the name of the poet. The Swinburne line is :

> I shall remember while the light lives yet,
> And in the night time I shall not forget.

Here I print a number of these sad, brave quotations taken at random, mostly from *The Times*, as they show the kind of poetry with which the bereaved console themselves. It will be noticed that the first three extracts are by Tennyson, Kipling and Rupert Brooke :

> Ah, Christ, that it were possible
> For one short hour to see
> The souls we loved, that they might tell us
> What and where they be.

> E'en as he trod that day to God so walked he from his birth
> In gentleness and simpleness, and honour and clean mirth.

> We have built a house that is not for Time's throwing,
> We have gained a peace, unshaken by pain for ever.

The following was quoted three times in one day, twice in *The Times* and once in *The Morning Post* :

> Seek him, thou sun, in the dread wilderness,
> For that he loved thee seek thou him, and bless
> His upturned face with one divine caress.
> Lightly, thou wind over his dear young head
> Whispering a benediction for the dead.

Among others that I have preserved are :

> Rest well, dear son, for at the Great Awakening,
> When Christ shall call His Soldiers to His side—
> His promise stands ; there shall be no forsaking
> Of those who fought for Him, and fighting died.

> Time would have brought him in her patient ways—
> So his young life spoke—to prosperous days.

To fulness of authority and praise
He would not wait so long.   A boy, he spent
His boy's dear life for England.   Be content ;
No honour of age had been more excellent.

———

The great Intelligences fair
That range above our mortal state,
In circle round the blessed gate,
Received and gave him welcome there.

———

He, too, loved life, but loving dared not save himself
Lest those that loved him should pay the price ;
Sunshine and youth and laughter—all he gave in sacrifice.

———

Fly, envious time, till thou run out thy race,

*   *   *   *   *

Then long Eternity shall greet our bliss
With an individual kiss.

———

She sought him among the dying,
She found him among the dead ;
The rose was still in his helmet,
But his life had stained it red.

———

Went the day well ?
We died and never knew—
But well or ill,
England, we died for you.

This of a child :

Blessed are thou whose childish feet
Stray where the living waters flow.

And this of Airmen :

Per ardua ad astra.

The following was published by an American woman,

Phoebe Crosley Allmuth, in *The New Republic*, during the war, when kings were toppling from their thrones :

> What is this talk of overthrowing kings ?
> Monstrous !
> Have we not all smelt rain
> On new ploughed earth ?
> Are we not all kings ?

*　　*　　*　　*　　*

Have I made it clear what I mean by a *Second Best Poem* ? A few of the 100 examples that follow I should probably include in an Anthology of *Best* Poetry. As for the others—the majority—if I had another year in which to compile this Anthology, I should be deleting and adding the whole time. Already I have a number thrust into a portfolio labelled " Must go in."

If I were forced to supply a definition of a Second Best Poem I would say it is one that a reader likes, not because he has been told to like it, but because he loves it. He keeps it by him : it helps him to live.

C. LEWIS HIND.

I
LOVE IS ENOUGH

LEAN HARD.

CHILD of My love, " Lean Hard,"
    And let me feel the pressure of thy care.
I know thy burden, child ; I shaped it,
Poised it in Mine own hand, made no proportion
Of its weight to thine unaided strength ;
For even as I laid it on I said—
" I shall be near, and while she leans on Me,
This burden shall be Mine, not hers ;
So shall I keep My child within the circling arms
Of Mine own love. Here lay it down, nor fear
To impose it on a shoulder which upholds
The government of worlds. Yet closer come,
Thou art not near enough ; I would embrace thy care,
So I might feel My child reposing on My breast.
Thou lovest Me ? I know it. Doubt not then,
But, loving Me, lean hard.

CHARLOTTE BICKERSTETH WARD.

Mrs. Charlotte Bickersteth Ward, sister of the late Bishop of Exeter and wife of the Rev. F. Ward, of Horndean, Hants, wrote " Lean Hard " after hearing a young girl say to an aged woman walking by her side, " Lean on me—lean hard." The incident occurred on a hill road in Switzerland. The lines, picked up accidentally by the Rev. G. Husband, in Folkestone, inspired a sermon delivered in the Parish Church of that town in 1871.

The following letter appeared in " The Times Literary Supplement," Feb. 26, 1925.

A QUERY.

Sir,—Could you or any reader give me some information about a poem entitled " Lean Hard," the first line of which runs as follows :—" Child of My Love, Lean Hard " ? The poem has been translated into Dutch, and is of some importance in connexion with the biography of the late Dr. Kuyper, the famous Dutch statesman. If, through your paper, I could find the original, and the name of its author, I should feel very much obliged.

W. A. VAN DONGEN, Sr.

49c, Lischstraat, Rotterdam.

JENNY KISS'D ME.

JENNY kiss'd me when we met,
     Jumping from the chair she sat in ;
Time, you thief, who love to get
Sweets into your list, put that in !
Say I'm weary, say I'm sad,
Say that health and wealth have miss'd me,
Say I'm growing old, but add,
     Jenny kiss'd me.

LEIGH HUNT.

WHAT MY LOVER SAID

BY the merest chance, in the twilight gloom,
  In the orchard path he met me ;
In the tall, wet grass, with its faint perfume,
And I tried to pass, but he made no room,
  Oh, I tried, but he would not let me.
So I stood and blushed till the grass grew red,
  With my face bent down above it,
While he took my hand as he whispering said—
(How the clover lifted each pink, sweet head,
To listen to all that my lover said ;
  Oh, the clover in bloom, I love it !)

Had he moved aside but a little way,
  I could surely then have passed him ;
And he knew I never could wish to stay,
And would not have heard what he had to say,
  Could I only aside have cast him.
It was almost dark, and the moments sped,
  And the searching night wind found us,
But he drew me nearer and softly said—
(How the pure, sweet wind grew still, instead,
To listen to all that my lover said ;
  Oh, the whispering wind around us !)

I am sure that he knew when he held me fast,
  That I must be all unwilling ;
For I tried to go, and I would have passed,
As the night was come with its dew, at last,
  And the sky with its stars was filling.

But he clasped me close when I would have fled,
    And he made me hear his story,
And his soul came out from his lips and said—
(How the stars crept out where the white moon led,
To listen to all that my lover said ;
    Oh, the moon and the stars in glory !)

HOMER GREENE.

" What My Lover Said " first appeared in the " New York Evening Post " in 1875.
*It was signed H.G.—who was Homer Greene, a student at Union College. In many quarters
the authorship was attributed (perhaps with winks) to Horace Greely—" a youthful effusion."*

Two stanzas omitted.

THE LOOK.

STREPHON kissed me in the spring,
    Robin in the fall,
But Colin only looked at me
    And never kissed at all.

Strephon's kiss was lost in jest,
    Robin's lost in play,
But the kiss in Colin's eyes
    Haunts me night and day.

SARA TEASDALE.

LOVE ME LITTLE—LOVE ME LONG

L OVE me little, love me long,
Is the burden of my song.
Love that is too hot and strong
  Burneth soon to waste.
Still I would not have thee cold,
Not too backward or too bold ;
Love that lasteth till 'tis old
  Fadeth not in haste.
Such the love that I would gain,
Such the love, I tell thee plain,
Thou must give, or woo in vain ;
So to thee farewell.

ANON., 1570.

THE TIME I'VE LOST IN WOOING.

THE time I've lost in wooing,
   In watching and pursuing
     The light that lies
     In woman's eyes,
Has been my heart's undoing.
Though Wisdom oft has sought me,
I scorn'd the lore she brought me.
     My only books
     Were woman's looks,
And folly's all they've taught me !

And are those follies going ?
And is my proud heart growing
     Too cold or wise
     For brilliant eyes
Again to set it glowing ?
No !—vain, alas ! th' endeavour
From bonds so sweet to sever—
     Poor Wisdom's chance
     Against a glance
Is now as weak as ever !

THOMAS MOORE.

SIDNEY DREW.

TO-DAY my children came to me ;
    " Sidney Drew's dead ! "
They said.

I hope that Sidney Drew can see,
Even from far eternity.
Beyond these pallid April skies,
The tribute of my children's eyes !

LEONORA SPEYER.

I MET AN OLD MAN.

I MET an old, old man down town to-day,
   His shoulders bent and tottering, his form
Like some tall tree, once kingly in its sway,
   But battling feebly now against the storm.
I helped him breast the traffic of the street,
   And safe across, he turned to me and said :
" God always sends a friend to guide my feet
   As he will guide my spirit when I'm dead."
And further on I met a crippled child.
   He stumbled, hast'ning swifter than his crutch.
But as I caught and helped him up he smiled
   And put my half-spoke pity to the touch.
" 'Twas just a slip," he said, " and mother says
   That when I slip and give myself a pain
It's 'cause I'm walking blind—but God always
   Will send a friend to pick me up again."

JOHN W. LOW.

—From the *New York Evening Sun.*

AND YET I KNOW—

AND yet I know past all doubting, truly—
    And knowledge greater than grief can dim—
I know, as he loved, he will love me duly—
    Yea, better—e'en better than I love him.

And as I walk by the vast, calm river,
    The awful river so dread to see,
I say, " Thy breadth and thy depth for ever
    Are bridged by his thoughts that cross to me."

JEAN INGELOW.—From Divided.

OUTWITTED.

HE drew a circle that shut me out,
    Heretic, rebel, a thing to flout.
But love and I had the wit to win :
We drew a circle that took him in.

EDWIN MARKHAM.

II.

THE HOMELAND

THE STATELY HOMES OF ENGLAND.

THE stately homes of England,
  How beautiful they stand,
Amidst their tall ancestral trees,
  O'er all the pleasant land !
The deer across their greensward bound
  Through shade and sunny gleam,
And the swan glides past them with the sound
  Of some rejoicing stream.

The cottage homes of England
  By thousands on her plains,
They are smiling o'er the silvery brooks,
  And round the hamlet fanes.
Through glowing orchards forth they peep,
  Each from its nook of leaves,
And fearless there the lowly sleep,
  As the bird beneath their eaves.

The free fair homes of England,
  Long, long, in hut and hall,
May hearts of native proof be reared
  To guard each hallowed wall,
And green for ever be the groves,
  And bright the flowery sod,
Where first the child's glad spirit loves
  Its country and its God.

FELICIA HEMANS.

Two stanzas omitted.

I REMEMBER, I REMEMBER.

I REMEMBER, I remember
　　The house where I was born,
The little window where the sun
　　Came peeping in at morn ;
He never came a wink too soon
　　Nor brought too long a day ;
But now, I often wish the night
　　Had borne my breath away.

I remember, I remember
　　The roses, red and white,
The violets, and the lily-cups—
　　Those flowers made of light !
The lilacs where the robin built,
　　And where my brother set
The laburnum on his birthday—
　　The tree is living yet !

I remember, I remember
　　Where I was used to swing,
And thought the air must rush as fresh
　　To swallows on the wing ;
My spirit flew in feathers then,
　　That is so heavy now,
And summer pools could hardly cool
　　The fever on my brow.

I remember, I remember
　　The fir trees dark and high ;
I used to think their slender tops
　　Were close against the sky ;

It was a childish ignorance,
  But now 'tis little joy
To know I'm farther off from Heaven
  Than when I was a boy.

THOMAS HOOD.

I'VE BEEN ROAMING.

I'VE been roaming—I've been roaming,
   Where the meadow dew is sweet,
And I'm coming—and I'm coming
   With its pearls upon my feet.

I've been roaming—I've been roaming
   O'er the rose and lily fair,
And I'm coming—and I'm coming
   With their blossoms in my hair.

I've been roaming—I've been roaming
   Where the honeysuckle sips,
And I'm coming—and I'm coming
   With its dew upon my lips.

I've been roaming—I've been roaming
   Over hill and over plain,
And I'm coming—and I'm coming
   To my bower back again.

ANON.

IN CITY STREETS.

YONDER in the heather there's a bed for sleeping,
    Drink for one athirst, ripe blackberries to eat ;
Yonder in the sun the merry hares go leaping,
    And the pool is clear for travel-wearied feet.

Sorely throb my feet, a-tramping London highways,
    (Ah, the springy moss upon a northern moor),
Through the endless streets, the gloomy squares and
        byways,
    Homeless in the City, poor among the poor !

London streets are gold—ah, give me leaves a-glinting
    'Midst grey dykes and hedges in the autumn sun !
London water's wine, poured out for all unstinting—
    God ! For the little brooks that tumble as they run !

Oh, my heart is fain to hear the soft wind blowing,
    Soughing through the fir-tops up on northern fells !
Oh, my eye 's an ache to see the brown burns flowing
    Through the peaty soil and tinkling heather-bells.

ADA SMITH.

49

D

ENGLAND.

(By an Australian on her first visit to the Motherland.)

I THOUGHT that when my stranger-eyes
   Beheld this dreamed-of treasure trove
With primrose-haunted memories,
With proud and daffodilling love
I'd laugh, and bare my head to English rains,
Run singing through the green of English lanes
And stooping by a hedge kiss the sweet earth
That gave my fathers birth.

But there's no laughter on my lips
Nor yet a song, but like a bird
Stumbling on beauty's soul there slips
Into my mouth a sobbing word—
England ! Her fields are furrowed in my heart,
Her rivers are the little tears that start
As to some shadow-quiet place I creep,
Like a shy child, to weep.

P.T.—From the *Morning Post.*

THE VILLAGE PITCH.

THEY had no grandstand or marquee,
    Bunting, or pots of palm :
There was a wealth of leafy tree
Behind the bowler's arm.

There were no score cards to be had,
Numbers on boards to scan ;
Only we saw the butcher's lad
Bowl out the laundryman.

Lord's and the Oval truly mean
Zenith of hard-bought fame,
But it was just a village green
Mothered and made the game.

G. D. MARTINEAU.—From *The Way of the South Wind*.

CANADIAN BOAT-SONG.

(From the Gaelic.)

L ISTEN to me, as when ye heard our father
  Sing long ago the song of other shores—
Listen to me, and then in chorus gather
 All your deep voices, as ye pull your oars :
   Chorus :
  Fair these broad meads—these hoary woods are grand ;
  But we are exiles from our fathers' land.

From the lone shieling of the misty island
 Mountains divide us, and the waste of seas—
Yet still the blood is strong, the heart is Highland,
 And we in dreams behold the Hebrides :
   Chorus :
  Fair these broad meads—these hoary woods are grand ;
  But we are exiles from our fathers' land.

We ne'er shall tread the fancy-haunted valley,
 Where 'tween the dark hills creeps the small clear
    stream,
In arms around the patriarch banner rally,
 Nor see the moon on royal tombstones gleam :
   Chorus :
  Fair these broad meads—these hoary woods are grand ;
  But we are exiles from our fathers' land.

When the bold kindred, in the time long-vanish'd,
   Conquer'd the soil and fortified the keep—
No seer foretold the children would be banish'd,
   That a degenerate Lord might boast his sheep :

      Chorus :

   Fair these broad meads—these hoary woods are grand ;
   But we are exiles from our fathers' land.

Come foreign rage—let Discord burst in slaughter !
   O then for clansman true, and stern claymore—
The hearts that would have given their blood like water,
   Beat heavily beyond the Atlantic roar :

      Chorus :

   Fair these broad meads—these hoary woods are grand ;
   But we are exiles from our fathers' land.

JOHN GALT (?)

"The Canadian Boat-Song" first appeared in "Blackwood's Magazine" in the "Noctes Ambrosianae" in September, 1829.

Messrs. Wm. Blackwood & Sons have kindly furnished the following information :—
"The authorship of the poem has never been definitely discovered, but a search through our letters revealed the fact that we received a letter from John Galt shortly before September, 1829, written from Canada, where he was at that time, in which he referred to an enclosure he was sending to the Editor. As it was the custom for Wilson, Lockhart and Hogg to incorporate contributions from other hands into the Noctes, there is no particular reason why 'The Canadian Boat Song' should not have been written by somebody other than these three ; and it is our opinion that the poem was written by John Galt, although up to the present we have never discovered more definite proof than what is referred to above.
"This poem is sometimes referred to as the 'Highland' Canadian Boat-Song, to prevent confusion with the title of Thomas Moore's poem."

The best known lines in Thomas Moore's "Canadian Boat-Song" are :—

      "Row brothers, row ! the stream runs fast,
      The rapids are near, and the daylight's past."

III.

ABOUT WOMEN

THE LASS OF RICHMOND HILL.

ON Richmond Hill there lives a lass
  More bright than May-day morn,
Whose charms all other maids surpass—
  A rose without a thorn.

This lass so neat, with smiles so sweet,
  Has won my right good-will ;
I'd crowns resign to call her mine,
  Sweet lass of Richmond Hill.

Ye zephyrs gay, that fan the air,
  And wanton through the grove,
Oh, whisper to my charming fair,
  I die for her I love !

How happy will the shepherd be
  Who calls this nymph his own !
Oh, may her choice be fix'd on me !
  Mine's fix'd on her alone.

—UPTON.

The music of this happy song was composed by the father of Theodore Hook. It was sung at " the convivial entertainments " at Vauxhall Gardens.

SHE WORE A WREATH OF ROSES.

SHE wore a wreath of roses that night when first we met,
    Her lovely face was smiling beneath her curls of jet ;
Her footsteps had the lightness, her voice the joyous tone,
The tokens of a youthful heart where sorrow is unknown.
I saw her but a moment, yet methinks I see her now,
With a wreath of summer flowers upon her snowy brow.

A wreath of orange flowers when next we met she wore,
The expression of her features was more thoughtful than
    before,
And standing by her side was one, who strove, and not
    in vain,
To soothe her leaving that dear home she ne'er might
    view again.
I saw her but a moment, yet methinks I see her now,
With a wreath of orange blossoms upon her snowy brow.

And once again I saw that brow, no bridal wreath was
    there,
The widow's sombre cap conceal'd her once luxuriant hair ;
She weeps in silent solitude, for there is no one near,
To press her hand within his own, and wipe away the tear !
I see her broken-hearted, and methinks I see her now,
In the pride of youth and beauty, with a wreath upon
    her brow.

THOMAS HAYNES BAYLY.

THE OLD WOMAN.

I HAVE been loved.
    Once, long ago, I had so much to give ;
All Love's alluring subtleties I knew,
Warm raptures, and the tenderness that binds
The fiercer passions into lasting stuff.

I was a friend, I kept a burnished mind ;
No man could give men friendship quite so sweet,
So mother-comforting as mine !
And I could give the great gifts of the Gods ;
With sons I gave men Immortality.

Now I am old, I sit here quietly,
Calm in my corner with my memories.
Colour and warmth have left me, but I smile
My wise old smile, saying " I lived my life—
I have been loved."

Z. M. THORRE.—From the *Poetry Review*.

GOD DID NOT MAKE HER VERY WISE.

GOD did not make her very wise,
  But carved a strangeness round her mouth ;
He put great sorrow in her eyes,
And softness for men's souls in drouth,
And on her face, for all to see,
The seal of awful tragedy.

God did not make her very fair
But white and lithe and strange and sweet ;
A subtle fragrance in her hair,
A slender swiftness in her feet,
And in her hands a slow caress ;
God made these for my steadfastness.

God did not give to her a heart,
But there is that within her face
To make men long to muse apart
Until they goodness find and grace,
And think to read and worship there
All good : yet she is scarcely fair.

A. BERNARD MIALL.—From *The Academy*.

THE HAND OF THE FUTURE.

WHEN I can feel this little hand of thine
    Nestling beneath mine own, my Mother-heart
Rebukes itself : How can I be alarmed ?
How dare I fear ? 'Tis such a little hand,
All rough with play ! Years upon years must pass
Ere thou art grown : and with God's help and mine
Before thy hand doth equal mine in size
We shall have buckled on impregnable
And shining armour ; and this hand shall wield
The broadsword of high virtue with such might
That not a caitiff tempter of them all
But shall be vanquished in the fray ; and yet
I am thy Mother, and this heart that shakes
With fear for what the future holds, is but
The heart that swelled with anguish and with pride
When thou wert given first to me.   I know
How good a thing is knowledge ; and how right
It is that man shall try his strength alone
And take his chance against the foes that press :
But, ah ! I'd shield thee if I could—would give
My very life itself if it would serve.

Dear little hand, when thou art twice this size
Wilt thou still fold thy mate in prayer should she
Who kneels here now have passed away and gone ?
Keep thyself clean, for in thy hollowed palm
Rests, oh, my son, thy Mother's anxious heart !

CAROLINE RUSSELL BISPHAM.

The little boy grew to be a man and died for England in 1917, aged nineteen years.

THE MOTHER SUPERIOR.

I WENT shopping in New York
   With the Mother Superior.
Before we left the great door of the convent
The Reverend Mother, very stately,
Gave her final orders to the Sisters.
They listened in obedience—
They each made a reverence as we passed.

And then we took a Broadway car.
The conductor called to her to step lively.
The crowd shoved her to a seat.
Suddenly
She had become
Only a sweet-faced, frightened old woman
Wrapped in black cloth.

JANE SHUBERT CLARK.—From *Touchstone* (*U.S.A.*)

SOUTHERNWOOD.

SO I have harvested my womanhood
   Into one tall green bush of southernwood ;
And if the leaves are green about your feet,
And if my fragrance on a day should meet
And brace your weariness, why, not in vain
Shall I have husbanded from sun and rain
My spices if you chance to find them sweet.

I have grown up beneath the sheltering shade
Of roses ; roses poignant scents have made
My sharp spice sweeter than 'twas wont to be.
Therefore, if any vagrant gather me
And wear me in his bosom, I will give
Him dreams of roses ; he shall dream and live,
And wake to find the rose a verity.

Gather me, gather. I have dreams to sell.
The sea is not by any fluted shell
More faithfully remembered, than I keep
My thoughts of roses, through beguiling sleep
And the bewildering day. I'll give to him
Who gathers me more sweetness than he'd dream
Without me—more than any lily could ;
I that am flowerless, being southernwood.

From the Pall Mall Gazette.

YET I KNOW THAT NOW.

YET I know that now I had answered " Yes "
    (Were I asked my will by the Father of All),
" I desire to be, I am glad to be born ! "
And all because on a soft May morn,
My neighbour's collie-dog, black and tan,
Leapt over the privet hedge, and ran
With a rush and a cry and a bound to my side.
And because I saw his master ride
Over the flaming yellow gorse.

LADY CURRIE, 1905.

LET ME GROW LOVELY.

LET me grow lovely, growing old ;
    So many old things do:
Laces and ivory and gold
And silks need not be new.

And there is healing in old trees,
Old streets a glamour hold,
Why may not I, as well as these,
Grow lovely, growing old ?

KARLE WILSON BAKER.

E

EMILY SPARKS.

WHERE is my boy, my boy—
    In what far part of the world?
The boy I loved the best of all in the school?—
I, the teacher, the old maid, the virgin heart,
Who made them all my children.
Did I know my boy aright,
Thinking of him as spirit aflame,
Active, ever aspiring?
Oh, boy, boy, for whom I prayed and prayed
In many a watchful hour at night,
Do you remember the letter I wrote you
Of the beautiful love of Christ?
And whether you ever took it or not,
My boy, wherever you are,
Work for your soul's sake,
That all the clay of you, all the dross of you,
May yield to the fire of you,
Till the fire is nothing but light? . . .
Nothing but light!

EDGAR LEE MASTERS.—From *The Spoon River Anthology.*

SANTA TERESA'S BOOKMARK

(From the Spanish of Santa Teresa).

LET nothing disturb thee,
  Nothing affright thee ;
All things are passing ;
God never changeth ;
Patient endurance
Attaineth to all things ;
Who God possesseth
In nothing is wanting ;
Alone God sufficeth.

H. W. LONGFELLOW.

IV.
ABOUT CHILDREN

BABY.

WHERE did you come from, baby dear ?
  Out of the everywhere into here.

Where did you get those eyes so blue ?
Out of the sky as I came through.

What makes the light in them sparkle and spin ?
Some of the starry twinkles left in.

Where did you get that little tear ?
I found it waiting when I got here.

What makes your forehead so smooth and high ?
A soft hand stroked it as I went by.

What makes your cheek like a warm white rose ?
I saw something better than anyone knows.

Whence that three-cornered smile of bliss ?
Three angels gave me at once a kiss.

Where did you get this pearly ear ?
God spoke, and it came out to hear.

Where did you get those arms and hands ?
Love made itself into bonds and bands.

Feet, whence did you come, you darling things ?
From the same box as the cherubs' wings.

How did they all just come to be you ?
God thought about me, and so I grew.

But how did you come to us, you dear ?
God thought about you, and so I am here.

GEORGE MACDONALD.

COME TO ME, O YE CHILDREN.

COME to me, O ye children !
    For I hear you at your play,
And the questions that perplexed me
    Have vanished quite away.

        *   *   *   *

Come to me, O ye children !
    And whisper in my ear
What the birds and the winds are singing
    In your sunny atmosphere.

For what are all our contrivings,
    And the wisdom of our books,
When compared with your caresses,
    And the gladness of your looks ?

Ye are better than all the ballads
    That ever were sung or said ;
For ye are living poems,
    And all the rest are dead.

H. W. LONGFELLOW.

Five stanzas omitted.

THE CHANGELING.

I HAD a little daughter,
    And she was given to me
To lead me gently backward
    To the heavenly Father's knee.
That I, by the force of nature,
    Might in some dim wise divine
The depth of His infinite patience
    To this wayward soul of mine.

I know not how others saw her,
    But to me she was wholly fair,
And the light of the heaven she came from
    Still lingered and gleamed in her hair ;
For it was as wavy and golden,
    And as many changes took,
As the shadows of sun-gilt ripples
    On the yellow bed of a brook.

To what can I like her smiling
    Upon me, her kneeling lover,
How it leaped from her lips to her eye-lids,
    And dimpled her wholly over,
Till her outstretched hands smiled also,
    And I almost seemed to see
The very heart of her mother
    Sending sun through her veins to me !

She had been with us scarce a twelve-month,
    And it hardly seemed a day,
When a troop of wandering angels
    Stole my little daughter away ;

Or perhaps those heavenly Zingari
   But loosed the hampering strings,
And when they had opened her cage-door,
   My little bird used her wings.

But they left in her stead a changeling,
   A little angel child,
That seems like her bud in full blossom,
   And smiles as she never smiled :
When I wake in the morning, I see it
   Where she always used to lie,
And I feel as weak as a violet
   Alone 'neath the awful sky ;

As weak, yet as trustful also ;
   For the whole year long I see
All the wonders of faithful Nature
   Still worked for the love of me ;
Winds wander, and dews drip earthward,
   Rain falls, suns rise and set,
Earth whirls, and all but to prosper
   A poor little violet.

This child is not mine as the first was,
   I cannot sing it to rest,
I cannot lift it up fatherly
   And bless it upon my breast ;
Yet it lies in my little one's cradle
   And sits in my little one's chair,
And the light of the heaven she's gone to
   Transfigures its golden hair.

JAMES RUSSELL LOWELL.

THE OLD BOX.

I FOUND an old box hid away in a room,
    And, lifting the lid open wide,
I found a little girl's pinafores hid,
And worn-out shoes tucked under the lid,
And tattered old toys inside.

Childhood's dreams all hidden away,
Bits from the "backwards" lane,
Headless dolls, and a ragged old goat,
And a choky feeling came into my throat ;
I wanted my pinnies again.

I found an old box all hidden away,
Oh, but those were the happiest days !
Pinnies all tattered and hair ribbons old,
But somehow I wonder if Heaven will hold
The key to my childhood's ways ?

ANON

IF MOTHER KNEW.

IF mother knew the way I felt—
  And I'm sure a mother should—
She wouldn't make it quite so hard
  For a person to be good !

I want to do the things she says ;
  I try to all day long ;
And then she just skips all the right,
  And pounces on the wrong !

A dozen times I do a thing,
  And one time I forget ;
And then she looks at me and asks
  If I can't remember yet ?

She'll tell me to do something,
  And I'll really start to go ;
But she'll keep right on telling it
  As if I didn't know,

Till it seems as if I couldn't—
  It makes me kind of wild ;
And then she says she never saw
  Such a disobliging child.

I go to bed all sorry,
  And say my prayers, and cry,
And mean next day to be so good
  I just can't wait to try.

And I get up next morning,
  And mean to do just right ;
But mother's sure to scold me
  About something before night.

I wonder if she really thinks
  A child could go so far,
As to be perfect all the time
  As the grown-up people are !

If she only knew I tried to—
  And I'm sure a mother should—
She wouldn't make it quite so hard
  For a person to be good !

ANON.

THE CHILDREN.

THEIRS are such tiny feet,
  They have gone so short way to meet
The years which are required to break
Their steps to evenness, and make them go
More sure and slow.

Theirs are such little hands !
Be kind ; things are so new, and life but stands
A step beyond the doorway.   All around
New day has found
Such tempting things to shine upon ; and so
The hands are tempted oft, you know.

Theirs are such fond clear eyes,
That widen to surprise
At every turn ! They are so often held
To sun or showers ; showers soon dispelled
By looking in our face.
Love asks, for such, much grace.

                                SARA M. B. PIATT

LITTLE.

WHEN God makes a lovely thing,
    The fairest and completest,
He makes it little, don't you know,
For little things are sweetest.

Little birds and little flowers,
Little diamonds, little pearls ;
But the dearest things on earth
Are the little boys and girls.

ANON.

TOMMY'S DEAD.

YOU may give over plough, boys,
    You may take the gear to the stead ;
All the sweat o' your brow, boys,
Will never get beer and bread.
The seed's waste, I know, boys ;
There's not a blade will grow, boys ;
'Tis cropped out, I trow, boys,
And Tommy's dead.

There's something not right, boys,
But I think it's not in my head ;
I've kept my precious sight, boys—
The Lord be hallowed.
Outside and in
The ground is cold to my tread,
The hills are wizen and thin,
The sky is shrivelled and shred ;
The hedges down by the loan
I count them bone by bone,
The leaves are open and spread.
But I see the teeth of the land,
And hands like a dead man's hand,
And the eyes of a dead man's head.
There's nothing but cinders and sand,
The rat and the mouse have fled,
And the summer's empty and cold ;
Over valley and wold,
Wherever I turn my head,

F

There's a mildew and a mould ;
The sun's going out overhead,
And I'm very old,
And Tommy's dead.

What am I staying for, boys ?
You're all born and bred—
'Tis fifty years and more, boys,
Since wife and I were wed ;
And she's gone before, boys,
And Tommy's dead.

SYDNEY DOBELL.

Portions omitted.

Sydney Dobell was born at Cranbrook, Kent, in 1824, and died at Nailsworth, Gloucester, in 1874. By profession he seems to have been a wine merchant at Cheltenham. A complete edition of his poetical works was published after his death. Literary editors are often asked who wrote—

> " *There's a mildew and a mould ;*
> *The sun's going out overhead,*
> *And I'm very old,*
> *And Tommy's dead.*"

DICKENS IN CAMP.

ABOVE the pines the moon was slowly drifting,
   The river sang below ;
The dim Sierras, far beyond, uplifting
   Their minarets of snow ;

The roaring camp-fire, with rude humour, painted
   The ruddy tints of health
On haggard face and form that drooped and fainted
   In the fierce race for wealth ;

Till one arose, and from his pack's scant treasure
   A hoarded volume drew,
And cards were dropped from hands of listless leisure
   To hear the tale anew ;

And then, while round them shadows gathered faster
   And as the fire-light fell,
He read aloud the book wherein the Master
   Had writ of " Little Nell " :

Perhaps 'twas boyish fancy,—for the reader
   Was youngest of them all,—
But, as he read, from clustering pine and cedar
   A silence seemed to fall ;

The fir-trees gathering closer in the shadows,
   Listened in every spray,
While the whole camp, with " Nell " on English
    meadows,
   Wandered and lost their way ;

And so in mountain solitudes—o'ertaken
    As by some spell divine—
Their cares dropped from them like the needles
      shaken
    From out the gusty pine.

Lost is that camp, and wasted all its fire ;
    And he who wrought that spell ?—
Ah, towering pine and stately Kentish spire,
    Ye have one tale to tell !

Lost is that camp ! but let its fragrant story
    Blend with the breath that thrills
With hop-vines' incense all the pensive glory
    That fills the Kentish hills.

And on that grave where English oak and holly
    And laurel wreaths entwine,
Deem it not all too presumptuous folly,—
    This spray of Western pine !

BRET HARTE.

John Forster, in his " Life of Charles Dickens," writes :—

" *Not many months before my friend's death he had sent me two ' Overland Monthlies' containing two sketches by a young American writer, Bret Harte, far away in California, ' The Luck of Roaring Camp,' and ' The Outcasts of Poker Flat.' . . . . I have rarely known him (Charles Dickens) more honestly moved. A few months passed ; telegraph wires flashed over the world that he had passed away on the 9th of June ; and the young writer of whom he had then written to me, all unconscious of that praise, put his tribute of gratefulness and sorrow into the form of a poem called ' Dickens In Camp.' *"

V.

NATURE

GOD'S GARDEN.

THE Lord God planted a garden
    In the first white days of the world,
And He set there an angel warden
    In a garment of light unfurled.

So near the peace of Heaven
    The hawk might meet with the wren,
For there in the cool of the even
    God walked with the first of men.

And I dream that those garden closes,
    With their glades and their sun-flecked sod,
And their lilies and bowers of roses,
    Were laid by the hand of God.

The kiss of the sun for pardon,
    The song of the birds for mirth—
One is nearer God's Heart in a garden
    Then anywhere else on earth.

DOROTHY FRANCES GURNEY.

This poem was written in the late Lord Ronald Gower's visitors' book, and was inspired by his garden at Hammerfield, Penshurst.

THE OLD NURSE.

AND Nature, the old nurse, took
   The child upon her knee,
Saying : " Here is a story book
   Thy Father has written for thee."

" Come wander with me," she said
   " Into regions yet untrod ;
And read what is still unread
   In the manuscripts of God."

And he wandered away and away
   With nature, the dear old nurse,
Who sang to him night and day
   The rhymes of the universe.

And whenever the way seemed long,
   Or his heart began to fail,
She would sing a more wonderful song
   Or tell a more marvellous tale.

H. W. LONGFELLOW.

—From *The Fiftieth Birthday of Agassiz.*

Stanzas omitted.

" AS SURE AS GOD MADE LITTLE APPLES."

WHEN God had made the oak trees
        And the beeches and the pines,
And the flowers and the grasses,
    And the tendrils of the vines,
He saw that there was wanting
A something in his plan,
    And He made the little apples,
    The little cider apples ;
    The sharp, sour, cider apples,
To prove His love for man.

ANON.

THE ROADMAN.

OLD Road, you've led me through a heap o' miles,
　　I guess we know each other pretty well ;
I've whistled to you, sung you songs o' night ;
　　You've told me mostly—all you've got to tell.

A queer old place the world must look to you
　　Who only see the underside of things,
The soles o' boots,—dogs' neatly cushioned paws,
　　Patched rubber tyres, an' wheezin' carriage
　　　　springs.

I've got me front an' back, me up an' down,
　　Your flat old face lies wrinklin' at the sun,
You climb, but never get above the ground,
　　Earth's still a-clutchin' you, when all is done.

There's times I've seen blue smoke between the trees
　　Like twistin' highways beckon as I pass.
I reckon it's the ghost o' some old road
　　That, left deserted, shuffled back to grass.

I like to think it's dawdlin' to the stars,
　　Seein' life proper, free as birds on wings,—
Old Road, I guess one day, like you, we'll find
　　We've only known the underneath o' things.

P. M. BOND.

IF I HAD A GOWN TO WEAR.

OH, if I had a gown to wear,
    I'd wear it up in London Town ;
And it should speak to Satin-Cheek,
To Golden-Gown, and Silver-Gown,
And it should tell to Dancing-Shoes
The village and the country news.

Oh, if I had a broom to cry,
I'd cry it in the country ways ;
" Oh, buy a broom and sweep your room
With country nights and country days,
With coolness from the country streams,
And fragrance that is good for dreams."

Oh, if I had a song to sing,
I'd sing it up in London Town ;
And it should bear to Worse-of-Wear
To Lightly-Lie and Low-Lie-Down,
The easement of the country hills,
And pleasuring from daffodils.

AGNES GROZIER HERBERTSON.

—From the Daily Chronicle.

THE COUNTRYMAN.

I AM sick of the sizzling arc-lights—I want a country
    moon ;
Your cities and towns they weary me, midnight or morn
    or noon.
I want the full moon o'er the tree-tops, in the whispering
    country night,
Instead of the brazen electric lamps with their blue and
    garish light—
           Oh ! I want to go home.

The scents of your pit-like streets appal a man with a heart,
And I will not famish here all my life—nor even a further
    part
Of my life. I long to break free from these dark and horrible
    dreams,
And in place of unmusical feminine mirth hear laughter
    of little streams—
           Oh ! I want to go home.

Machine-made airs of mechanical fans fail when the
    country breeze
Flies to my mind—the great, strong wind pouring through
    clean pine trees—
My ears are stunned with the vile cab-calls, shrill and
    piercing and long,
But I mask my face, though my heart cries out for the
    sound of a blackbird's song—
           Oh ! I want to go home.

Is there a man on the countryside who desires to return
    to the town ?
I ask for unfeasible things—but how swiftly I would go
    down
Exchanging with him the whole of my life, if I could, for
    a single year
In the places I know where the heather can grow and a
    city is nowhere near—
        Oh ! I want to go home.

BERTRAM ATKEY.—From the *Westminster Gazette*.

CONTENTMENT.

WHAT little things give you delight,
    A cottage white, a path to weed,
A tiny nest of fledgling wrens,
    And six brown hens to tend and feed ;

And new-born lambs on crooked legs,
    Blue thrushes' eggs, old water mills,
And frothy milk in brimming cans,
    And caravans, and dimpled hills ;

And when the shadows gold grow long,
    The blackbird's song begins to tire,
A corner in the ingle-nook,
    A poetry book beside the fire.

C. L. LANYON.—From the Observer.

" SOMEDAY."

" SOMEDAY, when I am growing tired of London's fret
      and cry,
I'll have a cottage by the sea and watch the ships go by,
With red-earthed, heath'ry hills behind, and green cliffs
      at my door,
A little winding ribbon road, and creamy, wave-kissed
      shore.
And in my garden I will grow all kinds of lovely things,
An apple tree, and gilly flowers, and clematis that clings :
A hedge of yew, and rosemary, delphiniums, and phlox,
Forget-me-nots, and lavender, and rows of hollyhocks :
And in a corner tucked away, all feath'ry green and blue,
The little flower that tears my heart, love-in-a-mist, and
      rue.

And so one day, when I have spent my passion and my pain
In tears and work in London Town, and found my Peace
      again,
Why then I'll wander ' down-along,' and on the cliffs will
      lie
Beside the rolling Western sea, and watch the ships go by.
And then, God grant, one blue-gold day, the fresh clean
      winds may free
The idle sails, and send my Love back Home again to me."

N. M. STEPHEN

THE FORGET-ME-NOT.

WHEN to the flowers beautiful
　　The Father gave a name,
Back came a little blue-eyed one
　　(All timidly it came) :
And standing at the Father's feet,
　　And gazing in His face,
It said in low and trembling tones,
　　With sweet and gentle grace,
" Dear God, the name Thou gavest me,
　　Alas ! I have forgot."
Then kindly looked the Father down,
　　And said, " Forget ME not."

ANON.

VI.

THE KNIGHT OF BETHLEHEM

THERE WAS A KNIGHT OF BETHLEHEM.

THERE was a Knight of Bethlehem,
  Whose wealth was tears and sorrows.
His men-at-arms were little lambs,
His trumpeters were sparrows.
His castle was a wooden cross,
Whereon he hung so high ;
His helmet was a crown of thorns
Whose crest did reach the sky.

HENRY NEVILLE MAUGHAM.
—From *The Husband of Poverty.*

MAGDALEN AT MICHAEL'S GATE.

MAGDALEN at Michael's gate
    Tirled at the pin,
On Joseph's thorn sang the blackbird—
    " Let her in, let her in ! "

" Hast thou seen the wounds ? " said Michael ;
    " Knowest thou thy sin ? "
" It is evening," sang the blackbird,
    " Let her in, let her in ! "

" Yes, I have seen the wounds,
    And I know my sin."
" She knows it well," sang the blackbird,
    " Let her in, let her in ! "

" Thou bring'st no offerings ! " said Michael,
    " Naught save sin ! "
" She is sorry ! " sang the blackbird,
    " Let her in, let her in ! "

When he had sung himself to sleep,
    And night did begin ;
ONE came and opened Michael's gate,
    And Magdalen went in.

HENRY KINGSLEY.

A BALLAD OF TREES AND THE MASTER.

INTO the woods my Master went,
  Clean forspent, forspent.
Into the woods my Master came
Forspent with love and shame.
But the olives they were not blind to Him,
And the little grey leaves were kind to Him,
The thorn-tree had a mind to Him
When into the woods He came.

Out of the woods my Master went,
And He was well content.
Out of the woods my Master came
Content with Death and Shame.
When Death and Shame would woo Him last
From under the trees they drew Him last,
'Twas on a tree they slew Him—last
When out of the woods He came.

SYDNEY LANIER.

An American poet and critic. In 1879 he was appointed lecturer on English literature at Johns Hopkins University, Baltimore.

ONCE AS HE STOOD—

ONCE as He stood beside her knee and read,
    She drew His lovely head
Close to her breast in mother-sweet embrace.
But as He raised His face
She saw the sudden tears that filled His eyes,
    And saddened with surprise.
Why should her little Son be moved like this
    At His fair mother's kiss ?

The long years passed.   Then fell the dolorous tide
    Shadowed and prophesied.
John entered trembling to the mother pale
And told the whole sad tale—
The garden scene, and the foul artifice
    Of the betrayer's kiss.
And so she understood, that night of woe,
    His tears of long ago.

        F. REYNOLDS.—From the *London Mercury*.

THE CROSS.

THERE was a cross on Calvary,
    And stark against the sky
There hung the Christ of all the world ;
    Men saw, and passed it by.

There is a cross on the wide downs,
    High on a hill it stands ;
And men have carved and placed it there
    With love-inspirèd hands.

They left Him dead on Calvary,
    But He is living still ;
His cross against an English sky—
    CHRIST—on a Sussex hill.

                          ENID CLAY.

" CHRISTMAS."

Written on H.M.S. " Iron Duke," 1914.

A BOY was born at Bethlehem
    That knew the haunts of Galilee,
He wandered on Mount Lebanon
   And learned to love each forest tree.

But I was born at Marlborough,
   And love the homely faces there ;
And for all other men besides
   'Tis little love I have to spare.

I should not mind to die for them,
   My own dear downs, my comrades true.
But that great heart of Bethlehem,
   He died for men he never knew.

And yet, I think, at Golgotha,
   As Jesus' eyes were closed in death,
They saw with love most passionate
   The village street at Nazareth.

E. HILTON YOUNG, M.P.—From *A Muse at Sea.*

I ONCE MET A KIND MAN.

I ONCE met a kind man
    Who laughed with me,
I'd have liked him for a brother,
    For his jollity.

He mentioned Beersheba
    And Galilee,
And other places lying deep
    In the cool country.

A little boy told me,
    Stopping in his play,
That it might have been Christ
    Who talked to me that day.

HAROLD LEWIS COOK.—From the *Westminster Gazette.*

VII.
RATHER SAD

LA VIE.

" LA vie est vaine,
    Un peu d'amour,
Un peu de haine
Et puis—bonjour !

La vie est brève,
Un peu d'espoir,
Un peu de rêve,
Et puis—bonsoir ! "

Léon Montenaeken.

Many have attempted a translation, or a free adaptation of this little poem. Perhaps the nearest to the spirit of its meaning, with differences, is that which George du Maurier printed on the last page of "Trilby."

A LITTLE work, a little play
    To keep us going—and so, good-day !

A little warmth, a little light
Of love's bestowing—and so, good-night !

A little fun to match the sorrow
Of each day's growing—and so, good-morrow !

A little trust that when we die
We reap our sowing ! And so, good-bye !

ILLUSION.

GOD and I in space alone,
   And nobody else in view,
And "Where are the people, O Lord?" I said,
"The earth below, and the sky o'er head
   And the dead whom I once knew?"

"That was a dream," God smiled and said,
   "A dream that seemed to be true.
There are no people, living or dead,
   There is nothing but Me and you."

"Why do I feel no fear?" I asked,
   "Meeting you here this way.
That I have sinned I know full well;
And is there a heaven and is there a hell,
   And is this the Judgment Day?"

"Nay, those were but dreams," the great God said
   "Dreams that have ceased to be;
There are no such things as sin and fear,
There is no you; you never have been:
   There is nothing at all but ME."

This poem, signed "An American Brahmacharini," appeared in "Prabuddha Bharata."

THE OLD FAMILIAR FACES.

I HAVE had playmates, I have had companions,
    In my days of childhood, in my joyful schooldays,
All, all are gone, the old familiar faces.

I have been laughing, I have been carousing,
Drinking late, sitting late, with my bosom cronies,
All, all are gone, the old familiar faces.

I loved a love once, fairest among women ;
Closed are her doors on me, I must not see her—
All, all are gone, the old familiar faces.

I have a friend, a kinder friend has no man ;
Like an ingrate, I left my friend abruptly ;
Left him, to muse on the old familiar faces.

Ghost-like, I paced round the haunts of my childhood.
Earth seemed a desert I was bound to traverse,
Seeking to find the old familiar faces.

Friend of my bosom, thou more than a brother,
Why wert not thou born in my father's dwelling ?
So might we talk of the old familiar faces—

How some they have died, and some they have left me,
And some are taken from me ; all are departed ;
All, all are gone, the old familiar faces.

CHARLES LAMB.

I HAVE A DREAM.

I HAVE a dream—that some day I shall go
    At break of dawn adown a rainy street,
A grey old street, and I shall come in the end
To the little house I have known, and stand; and you,
Mother of mine, who watch and wait for me,
Will you not hear my footstep in the street,
And, as of old, be ready at the door,
To give me rest again ? . . . I shall come home.

H. D. LOWRY.—From *The Hundred Windows.*

H. D. Lowry died young. He was a Cornishman, came to London, published a book of poems called " The Hundred Windows," did good work for the " Morning Post " and the " National Observer,"—and then—Good-night,

NOW THAT MY LOVES LIES SLEEPING.

NOW that my love lies sleeping
　　How call me glad or sad,
Who gave into her keeping
　　Everything I had—-

All love I held for beauty
　　And all I knew of truth,
All care for any duty,
　　And what I kept of youth ?

Now that my love lies sleeping
　　There's neither good nor bad,
I gave into her keeping
　　Everything I had.

H. D. LOWRY.—From *The Hundred Windows*.

H

I HAVE DESIRED TO GO.

I HAVE desired to go
  Where springs not fail.
To fields where flies no sharp and sided hail
And a few lilies blow.

And I have asked to be
Where no storms come,
Where the green swell is in the havens dumb
And out of the swing of the sea.

FATHER HOPKINS.

Subject: A Nun about to take the veil.

IF I SHOULD DIE TO-NIGHT.

IF I should die to-night,
   My friends would look upon my quiet face
Before they laid it in its resting place,
And deem that death had left it almost fair ;
And, laying snow-white flowers against my hair,
Would smooth it down with tearful tenderness,
And fold my hands with lingering caress,
Poor hands, so empty and so cold to-night !

   If I should die to-night,
My friends would call to mind, with loving thought
Some kindly deed the icy hands had wrought ;
Some gentle word the frozen lips had said ;
Errands on which the willing feet had sped ;
The memory of my selfishness and pride,
My hasty words, would all be put aside,
And so I should be loved and mourned to-night.

   If I should die to-night,
Even hearts estranged would turn once more
    to me,
Recalling other days remorsefully.
The eyes that chill me with averted glance,
Would look upon me as of yore perchance
And soften, in the old, familiar way
For who could war with dumb, unconscious clay ?
So I might rest, forgiven of all, to-night.

Oh, friends, I pray to-night,
Keep not your kisses from my dead, cold brow,
The way is lonely, let me feel them now,
Think gently of me ; I am travel-worn ;
My faltering feet are pierced with many a thorn.
Forgive, oh hearts estranged, forgive, I plead !
When dreamless rest is mine I shall not need
The tenderness for which I long to-night.

ARABELLA EUGENIA SMITH.

This poem, by an American author, Arabella Eugenia Smith, had a run of publicity in the " Nineties." Rider Haggard quoted it in one of his novels, and, by some mischance let it be inferred that he was the author. He explained and expressed his regret in the " Pall Mall Gazette " when W. T. Stead was editor.

PAGEANT.

THOUGH I go by with banners,
    Oh, never envy me
These flags of scarlet flying,
    This purple that you see . . .

This air of marching triumph
    Was all that I could save
Of loves that had an ending
    And hopes that had a grave.

MARGARET WIDDEMER.—From the American *Outlook*.

AN EPITAPH.

HERE do I lie in faith !
    Not that God's purposes were clear to me ;
   Not that I read old books, and said, " I see !
Curst be the fool whose eyes are holden yet ! "
    But that I justified within my soul
    The Will that moved the worlds. It guides the whole ?
Let it this part remember or forget !

Here do I lie—in hope !
    Not that I say, " I kept my foot from sin ;
   Not that I think, or wish, to enter in
Where aureoled saints with new-born children rest ;
    But that no fellow-man can say of me,
    " I fell, and it was pleasing unto thee ;
Thine eyes behold despair, and acquiesced."

Here do I lie—and sleep !
    Sleep was the gift filched at my birth from me,
   But I inherit it eternally :
I close my hand on it, and now shall keep.
    Embraces of the flesh awakened " me " :
    Stripped of the flesh once more—and willingly—
In the embraces of the gods I sleep !

From the *Academy*, 1898

HOW HE DIED.

So he died for his faith. That is fine.
    More than most of us do.
But stay ; can you add to that line
    That he lived for it too ?

It is easy to die. Men have died
    For a wish or a whim—
From bravado, from passion or pride
    Was it harder for him ?

But to live ; every day to live out
    All the truth that he dreamt,
While his friends met his conduct with doubt,
    And the world with contempt—

Was it thus that he plodded ahead,
    Never turning aside ?
Then we'll talk of the life that he led,
    Never mind how he died.

E. CROSBY.

MY DEAREST DUST.

MY dearest dust, could not thy hasty day
    Afford thy drowsy patience leave to stay
One hour longer, so that we might either
Have set up, or gone to bed together ?
But since thy finished labour hath possessed
Thy weary limbs with early rest,
Enjoy it sweetly ; and thy widow bride,
Shall soon repose her by thy slumbering side :
Whose business now is only to prepare
My nightly dress and call to prayer.
Mine eyes wax heavy, and the days grow old—
The dew falls thick—my blood grows cold :—
Draw, draw the closed curtains, and make room,
My dear, my dearest dust, I come, I come.

From an Epitaph in a churchyard at Colneworth, Bedfordshire, on a magnificent monument erected in 1641 by Lady Dyer to her husband, whereon it says that they " multiplied themselves into 7 children."

I HAVE LIVED AND I HAVE LOVED.

I HAVE lived and I have loved ;
   I have waked and I have slept :
I have sung and I have danced ;
I have smiled and I have wept ;
I have won and wasted treasure ;
I have had my fill of pleasure ;
And all these things were weariness ;
And some of them were dreariness ;
And all these things—but two things ;—
Were emptiness and pain :
And Love it was the best of them—
And Sleep—worth all the rest of them.

L.S.—From the *Sydney Bulletin*.

SAY NOT, THE STRUGGLE NOUGHT AVAILETH.

SAY not, the struggle nought availeth,
   The labour and the wounds are vain,
The enemy faints not nor faileth,
   And as things have been they remain.

If hopes were dupes, fears may be liars ;
   It may be, in yon smoke concealed,
Your comrades chase e'en now the fliers,
   And, but for you, possess the field.

For while the tired waves, vainly breaking
   Seem here no painful inch to gain,
Far back, through creeks and inlets making,
   Comes silent, flooding in, the main.

And not by eastern windows only,
   When daylight comes, comes in the light ;
In front, the sun climbs slow—how slowly !
   But westward, look ! the land is bright.

ARTHUR HUGH CLOUGH

VIII.
WAR GAINS

THE BURIAL OF SIR JOHN MOORE

NOT a drum was heard, not a funeral note,
    As his corse to the rampart we hurried ;
Not a soldier discharged his farewell shot
    O'er the grave where our hero we buried.

We buried him darkly at dead of night,
    The sods with our bayonets turning ;
By the struggling moonbeam's misty light,
    And the lantern dimly burning.

No useless coffin enclosed his breast,
    Not in sheet nor in shroud we wound him ;
But he lay like a warrior taking his rest,
    With his martial cloak around him.

Few and short were the prayers we said,
    And we spoke not a word of sorrow ;
But we steadfastly gazed on the face that was dead,
    And we bitterly thought of the morrow.

We thought as we hollowed his narrow bed,
    And smoothed down his lonely pillow
That the foe and the stranger would tread o'er his head,
    And we far away on the billow !

Lightly they'll talk of the spirit that's gone,
    And o'er his cold ashes upbraid him,—
But little he'll reck, if they'll let him sleep on
    In the grave where a Briton has laid him.

But half our heavy task was done,
    When the clock struck the hour for retiring ;
And we heard the distant and random gun
    That the foe was sullenly firing.

Slowly and sadly we laid him down,
    From the field of his fame fresh and gory ;
We carved not a line, and we raised not a stone—
    But we left him alone with his glory.

CHARLES WOLFE.

KITCHENER.

NO man in England slept the night he died :
    The harsh, stern spirit passed without a pang,
And freed of mortal clogs his message rang.
In every wakeful mind the challenge cried :
Think not of me : one servant less or more
Means nothing now : hold fast the greater thing—
Strike hard, love truth, serve England and the King !

Servant of England, soldier to the core,
What does it matter where his body fall ?
What does it matter where they build his tomb ?
Five million men, from Calais to Khartoum,
These are his wreath and his memorial.

CHRISTOPHER MORLEY.—From *Songs for a Little House.*

First published in the American journal " Life."

IN FLANDERS FIELDS.

IN Flanders fields the poppies blow
  Between the crosses, row and row,
 That mark our place ; and in the sky
 The larks still bravely singing, fly
Scarce heard amid the guns below.

We are the Dead.   Short days ago
We lived, felt dawn, saw sunset glow,
  Loved and were loved, and now we lie
    In Flanders fields.

    *   *   *   *   *

To you from failing hands we throw
  The torch ; be yours to hold it high !
  If ye break faith with us who die
We shall not sleep, though poppies grow
    In Flanders fields.

JOHN McCRAE.—From *In Flanders Fields.*

This famous poem was written by Lieut.-Colonel John McCrae, of the Canadian Army.   A graduate in medicine of Toronto University he was appointed January 5, 1918, Consulting Physician to the British Armies in France and died in hospital January 28, 1918 " dark to the triumph which he died to gain."

OBITUARY.

In loving memory of———, who was killed in action
———, aged 20 years.

A LITTLE while—your grave will be o'ertrodden,
    Soon the frail cross have fallen in the breeze.
No loving hands are there to tend and cherish
That grave in foreign soil beyond the seas.
" Somewhere in France "—oh, surely, my beloved,
Tho' sign and token all be swept away,
It is not in that land of desolation,
But in my heart that you will rest alway.

From a London Newspaper.

I

SUDDENLY ONE DAY.

SUDDENLY one day
The last ill shall fall away.
The last little beastliness that is in our blood
Shall drop from us as the sheath drops from the bud,
And the great spirit of man shall struggle through
And spread huge branches underneath the blue.
In any mirror, be it bright or dim,
Man will see God staring back at him.

T. P. C. WILSON.—From the *Westminster Gazette.*

Found in the pocket of Capt. T. P. C. Wilson, killed in action.

SPORTSMEN IN PARADISE.

THEY left the fury of the fight
　　And they were tired.
The gates of Heaven were open quite,
　　Unguarded and unwired.
There was no sound of any gun,
　　The land was still and green ;
Wide hills lay silent in the sun,
　　Blue valleys slept between.

They saw far off a little wood
　　Stand up against the sky.
Knee-deep in grass a great tree stood—
　　Some lazy cows went by.
There were some rooks sailed overhead,
　　And once a church-bell pealed
" God ! but it's England," someone said,
　　" And there's a cricket-field ! "

" TIPUCA " (T. P. C. Wilson).—From the *Westminster Gazette.*

THE LITTLE GREY MULE.

NO one asked what he thought of war,
    How his conscience stood or anything more,
But they took him to France, to stand his chance,
    It's all right—only a mule.

He pulled his load to the top of the hill,
A shot rang out, and he lay quite still,
" Any one hit ? "   " No, we're quite fit,"
    It's all right—only a mule.

There is a field where the grass is long,
And God at the gate to right the wrong,
You can hear Him say, if you pass that way,
    " He's all right—little grey mule."

A. P.—From the *Westminster Gazette*.

IX.

PETITIONS, RESIGNATION AND COUNSEL

IN THINE OWN HEART.

THOUGH Christ a thousand times
  In Bethlehem be born,
If He's not born in thee,
  Thy soul is still forlorn.
The cross on Golgotha
  Will never save thy soul ;
The cross in thine own heart
  Alone can make thee whole.

Whate'er thou lovest, man,
  That too, become thou must ;
God, if thou lovest God,
  Dust, if thou lovest dust.
Go out, God will go in,
  Die thou, and let Him live.
Be not, and He will be,
  Wait, and He'll all things give.

To bring thee to thy God
  Love takes the shortest route ;
The way which knowledge leads
  Is but a round-about.
Drive out from thee the world,
  And then like God thou'lt be.
A heaven within thyself
  In calm eternity.

Let but thy heart, oh man,
  Become a valley low
And God shall rain on it,
  Till it will overflow.

Oh shame ! The silkworm works
  And spins till it can fly,
And thou, my soul, wilt still
  On thine old earth-clod lie ?

Man, if the time on earth
  Should seem too long for thee,
Turn thou to God and live
  Time-free, eternally.

ANGELUS SILESIUS.

The complete poem, as above, was reprinted some years ago in the Boston " Transcript."
The lines most often quoted are the first four of the second stanza.

GRANT, O GOD, THY PROTECTION.

GRANT, O God ! thy protection ;
   And in protection, strength ;
And in strength, understanding ;
And in understanding, knowledge ;
And in knowledge, knowledge of the truth ;
And knowing the truth, to love it ;
And when loving, to love all being ;
And in all Being, to love God ;
   God and all Goodness.

The Invocation at the opening of the Eisteddfod, Wales.   Translated by the Recorder of the Gorsedd, B. G. Evans, Carnarvon.

BRAHMA.

IF the Red Slayer think he slays,
   Or if the slain think he is slain,
They know not well the subtle ways
   I keep, and pass, and turn again.

Far or forgot to me is near ;
   Shadow and sunlight are the same ;
The vanished gods to me appear ;
   And one to me are shame and fame.

They reckon ill who leave me out ;
   When me they fly, I am the wings,
I am the doubter and the doubt,
   And I the hymn the Brahmin sings.

The strong gods pine for my abode,
   And pine in vain the sacred seven ;
But thou, meek lover of the good !
   Find me, and turn thy back on heaven.

RALPH WALDO EMERSON.

JIM BLUDSO.

HE never funked and he never lied
I reckon he never knowed how . . .

He weren't no saint—but at jedgment
I'd run my chance with Jem,
'Longside some pious gentlemen
That wouldn't shook hands with him.

He seen his duty, a dead-sure thing—
And went for it thar and then ;
And Christ ain't a-going to be too hard
On a man that died for men.

JOHN HAY.—From *Jim Bludso.*

RESIGNATION.

THERE is no flock, however watched and tended,
　　But one dead lamb is there !
There is no fireside, howsoe'er defended
　　But has one vacant chair !

The air is full of farewells to the dying,
　　And mournings for the dead ;
The heart of Rachael, for her children crying,
　　Will not be comforted !

Let us be patient ! These severe afflictions
　　Not from the ground arise,
But oftentimes celestial benedictions
　　Assume this dark disguise.

We see but dimly through the mists and vapours ;
　　Amid these earthly damps
What seem to us but sad, funereal tapers
　　May be heaven's distant lamps.

There is no death ! What seems so is transition ;
　　This life of mortal breath
Is but a suburb of the life elysian,
　　Whose portal we call death.

She is not dead—the child of our affection—
　　But gone unto that school
Where she no longer needs our poor protection,
　　And Christ himself doth rule.

H. W. LONGFELLOW.

Stanzas omitted.

A PRAYER TO OUR LADY.

LOOK kindly where poor people are,
    Mary of Homes, keep trouble far.

Shelter beneath thy prayers' wings
Mary of Roses, all young things.

Keep children warm thro' winds and rains
Of cold nights, Mary of Counterpanes.

Send us high skies, blue days and fair,
Mary of Swallows, bless the air.

Pray for the sea with pleading lips,
Make storms still, Mary of Ships.

Bring whalers home from Iceland seas
To their port, Mary of Oranges.

Paint lover's days a rose-red hue
Mary of Peacocks, green and blue.

All wandering men abroad at night
Mary of Candles, give them light.

Make a wide space behind their bars
For prisoners, Mary of the Stars.

Give lightsome hearts to folk that toil
And shining faces, Mary of Oil.

To mourners meek, that seek thy shrine
Give mirth for sadness, Mary of Wine.

Shed balm on aching eyes that weep
In woods of summer, Mary of Sleep.

Mary of Tyrol thy care be
For Flanders and for Brittany.

Send soon these weary wars may cease,
Mary of Jesu, give us peace.

Pray for me, as I ring thy chimes
In my poor belfry, Mary of Rhymes.

R. E. GALES (Rev.).—From *Skylark and Swallow*.

YESTERDAY NOW IS A PART OF FOREVER.

YESTERDAY now is a part of forever,
    Bound up in a sheaf, which God holds tight,
With glad days, and sad days, and bad days which never
Shall visit us more, with their bloom and their blight,
Their fulness of sunshine or sorrowful night.

Let them go, since we cannot re-live them,
Cannot undo and cannot atone—
God in his mercy receive, forgive them—
Only the new days are our own ;
To-day is ours, and to-day alone.

Every day is a fresh beginning ;
Listen, my soul, to the glad refrain :
And, spite of old sorrow and older singing,
And puzzles forecasted, and possible pain,
Take heart with the day, and begin again !

                                    SUSAN COOLIDGE.

WAITING.

SERENE, I fold my hands and wait,
  Nor care for wind, or tide, or sea ;
I rave no more 'gainst Time or Fate,
  For lo ! my own shall come to me.

I stay my haste, I make delays,
  For what avails this eager pace ?
I stand amid the eternal ways,
  And what is mine shall know my face.

Asleep, awake, by night or day,
  The friends I seek are seeking me ;
No wind can drive my bark astray,
  Nor change the tide of destiny. . . .

What matter if I stand alone ?
  I wait with joy the coming years ;
My heart shall reap where it hath sown,
  And garner up its fruit of tears.

The waters know their own and draw
  The brook that springs in yonder height ;
So flows the good with equal law
  Unto the soul of pure delight.

The stars come nightly to the sky ;
  The tidal wave unto the sea ;
Nor time, nor space, nor deep, nor high :
  Can keep my own away from me.

JOHN BURROUGHS.

X.

THE ETERNAL HOPE

O MAY I JOIN THE CHOIR INVISIBLE.

O MAY I join the choir invisible
   Of those immortal dead who live again
In minds made better by their presence. . . .

   This is life to come,
Which martyred men have made more glorious
For us who strive to follow.   May I reach
That purest heaven, be to other souls
The cup of strength in some great agony,
Enkindle generous ardour, feed pure love,
Beget the smiles that have no cruelty—
Be the sweet presence of a good diffused,
And in diffusion ever more intense.
So shall I join the choir invisible
Whose music is the gladness of the world.

GEORGE ELIOT.

OH, PERFECT RACE TO BE.

OH, perfect Race to be ! Oh, perfect Time !
    Maturity of Earth's unhappy youth !
Race whose undazzled eyes shall see the truth,
Made wise by all the errors of your prime !
Oh, Bliss and Beauty of the ideal Day !
Forget not, when your march has reached its goal,
The rich and reckless waste of heart and soul
You left so far behind you on your way !
Forget not, Earth, when thou shalt stretch thy hands
In blessing o'er thy happy sons and daughters,
And lift in triumph thy maternal head,
Circling the sun with music from all lands,
In anthems like the noise of many waters—
Forget not, Earth, thy disappointed Dead !
Forget not, Earth, thy disinherited !
Forget not the forgotten ! Keep a strain
Of divine sorrow in sweet undertone
For all the dead who lived and died in vain !
Imperial Future, when in countless train
The generations lead thee to thy throne,
Forget not the Forgotten and Unknown !

LOUISA SHORE.

EACH IN HIS OWN TONGUE.

A FIRE-MIST and a planet,
   A crystal and a cell,
A jelly-fish and a saurian,
   And caves where the cave-men dwell ;
Then a sense of law and beauty,
   And a face turned from the clod—
Some call it Evolution,
   And others call it God.

A haze on the far horizon,
   The infinite tender sky,
The ripe, rich tints of the cornfield,
   And the wild geese sailing high ;
And all over upland and lowland,
   The charm of the golden rod ;
Some of us call it Autumn,
   And others call it God.

Like tides on a crescent sea-beach,
   When the moon is new and thin,
Into our hearts high yearnings
   Come welling and surging in ;
Come from the mystic ocean,
   Whose rim no foot has trod—
Some of us call it Longing,
   And others call it God.

A picket frozen on duty,
   A mother starved for her brood,
Socrates drinking the hemlock,
   And Jesus on the Rood ;
And millions who, humble and nameless,
   The straight, hard pathway trod—
Some call it Consecration,
   And others call it God.

WILLIAM HERBERT CARRUTH (Dr.).

—From *Each in His Own Tongue. and Other Poems.*

EVOLUTION.

OUT of the dusk a shadow,
    Then a spark ;
Out of the cloud a silence,
Then a lark ;
Out of the heart a rapture,
Then a pain ;
Out of the dead, cold ashes,
Life again.

JOHN B. TABB.

THE MARSHES OF GLYNN.

A S the marsh-hen secretly builds on the watery sod,
     Behold I will build me a nest on the greatness of God ;
I will fly in the greatness of God as the marsh-hen flies
In the freedom that fills all the space twixt the marsh and
     the skies.
By so many roots as the marsh-grass sends in the sod
I will heartily lay me a-hold on the greatness of God :
Oh, like to the greatness of God is the greatness within
The range of the marshes, the liberal marshes of Glynn.

                                        SYDNEY LANIER.

Stanzas omitted. (See page 101.)

AT LAST.

WHEN on my day of life the night is falling,
  And, in the winds from unsunned spaces blown,
I hear far voices out of darkness calling
  My feet to paths unknown.

Thou, who hast made my home of life so pleasant,
  Leave not its tenant when its walls decay ;
O Love divine, O Helper ever present,
  Be Thou my strength and stay !

Be near me when all else is from me drifting :
  Earth, sky, home's pictures, days of shade and shine,
And kindly faces to my own uplifting
  The love which answers mine.

I have but Thee, O Father ! Let Thy Spirit
  Be with me then to comfort and uphold ;
No gate of pearl, no branch of palm, I merit,
  Nor street of shining gold.

Suffice it if—my good and ill unreckoned,
  And both forgiven through Thy abounding grace—
I find myself by hands familiar beckoned
  Unto my fitting place.

Some humble door among Thy many mansions,
  Some sheltering shade where sin and striving cease,
And flows for ever through heaven's green expansions
  The river of Thy peace.

There, from music round about me stealing,
  I fain would learn the new and holy song,
And find, at last, beneath Thy trees of healing,
  The life for which I long.

JOHN GREENLEAF WHITTIER.

THE GLEAM.

COMING we know not whence,
　Going we know not whither,
Lacking control, defence,
　Tossed here and drifting thither ;
The blind begetting the blind,
　The millions living for bread,
Grave-dust on the master-mind,
　The riddle for ever unread,
What proof in life, in death,
　That the soul has eternal breath ?

This ; on the night of the blind
　A burning and shining light !
This ; that a call may find
　The deaf in his own despite ;
A whisper may wake the sleeper,
　A thief be the foe of theft,
A sluggard his brother's keeper,
　A lover self-bereft ;
For nought but the spirit's asking
　A miser shall greatly give,
And, the god of his soul unmasking,
　A coward scorn to live.

This, this is our hope immortal,
　And this the gleam in the dark,
That a man will pass death's portal
　For love of that mystic spark !

F. H. FRIEDLAENDER.

IF LIFE WERE ALL.

IF life were all,
    Where were the recompense
For all our tears ?
The troubled toil
Of all the long-drawn years,
The struggle to survive
The passing show
Were scarce worth while,
    If life were all.

If life were all,
What were it worth to live ?
To build on pain,
So soon to learn
Our building were but vain,
And then to pass
To some vague nothingness
Were scarce worth while,
    If life were all.

If life were all,
How might we bear
Our poor heart's grief ?
Our partings frequent
And our pleasures brief,
The cup pressed to the lips,
Then snatched away,
Were scarce worth looking on
    If life were all.

Life is not all—
We build eternally,
And what is ours to-day
To make existence sweet
Is ours alway.
We stand on solid ground
That lasts for aye and aye,
And makes life's sojourn
Worth the while—
　　Life is not all.

　　Life is not all.
I do not know the plan :
I only know that God is good,
And that His strength sustains.
I only know that He is just ;
So in the starless, songless night
I lift my face and trust,
And God my spirit witness bears,
　　Life is not all.

HENRY C. WARNACK.

THE BLIND SPINNER

LIKE a blind spinner in the sun,
   I tread my days ;
I know that all the threads will run
   Appointed ways ;
I know each day will bring its task ;
And, being blind, no more I ask.

I do not know the use or name
   Of that I spin ;
I only know that someone came,
   And laid within
My hand the thread, and said, " Since you
Are blind, but one thing you can do."

Sometimes the threads so rough and fast
   And tangled fly,
I know wild storms are sweeping past,
   And fear that I
Shall fall, but dare not try to find
A safer place, since I am blind

*   *   *   *   *

     The hand divine
  I never doubt.
I know He set me here, and still,
And glad, and blind, I wait His will ;

But listen, listen, day by day,
    To hear their tread
Who bear the finished web away,
    And cut the thread,
And bring God's message in the Sun,
" Thou poor blind spinner, work is done."

HELEN HUNT JACKSON (American).

THE BURIAL OF MOSES.

BY Nebo's lonely mountain,
   On this side Jordan's wave,
In a vale in the land of Moab
   There lies a lonely grave.
And no man knows that sepulchre,
   And no man saw it e'er,
For the angels of God upturned the sod,
   And laid the dead man there.

That was the grandest funeral
   That ever passed on earth ;
But no man heard the trampling,
   Or saw the train go forth—
Noiselessly as the daylight
   Comes back when night is done,
And the crimson streak on ocean's cheek
   Grows into the great sun ;

Noiselessly as the spring-time
   Her crown of verdure weaves,
And all the trees on all the hills
   Open their thousand leaves ;
So without sound of music,
   Or voice of them that wept,
Silently down from the mountain's crown
   The great procession swept.

Perchance the bald old eagle,
　　On grey Beth-Peor's height,
Out of his lonely eyrie
　　Look'd on the wondrous sight ;
Perchance the lion stalking
　　Still shuns that hallow'd spot,
For beast and bird have seen and heard
　　That which man knoweth not.

　　　　*　　*　　*　　*　　*

Amid the noblest of the land
　　We lay the sage to rest,
And give the bard an honour'd place,
　　With costly marble drest,
In the great minster transept
　　Where lights like glories fall,
And the organ rings, and the sweet choir sings
　　Along the emblazoned wall.

This was the truest warrior
　　That ever buckled sword,
This the most gifted poet
　　That ever breath'd a word ;
And never earth's philosopher
　　Traced with his golden pen,
On the deathless page, truths half so sage
　　As he wrote down for men.

And had he not high honour,—
　　The hillside for a pall,
To lie in state while angels wait
　　With stars for tapers tall,
And the dark rock-pines, like tossing plumes,
　　Over his bier to wave,
And God's own hand in that lonely land,
　　To lay him in the grave ?

　　　　*　　*　　*　　*

O lonely grave in Moab's land !
  O dark Beth-Peor's hill !
Speak to these curious hearts of ours,
  And teach them to be still.
God hath His mysteries of grace,
  Ways that we cannot tell ;
He hides them deep, like the hidden sleep
  Of him He loved so well.

CECIL FRANCES ALEXANDER.

Stanzas ommitted.

BLACK AND WHITE.

"Though ye have lien among the pots, yet shall ye be as the wings of a dove, covered with silver."—Psalm LXVIII, v. 13.

THE lily holds its chalice white
  To gather city grime,
The snow, soft falling in the night,
  Is melted into slime ;
A black and sorry world is ours,
  The world of man's control,
For while he blackens flakes and flowers
  He smudges out his soul.

Yet are there dales where lilies keep
  Their goblets for the dew,
And holy hills that lie asleep
  In snow-sheets ever new ;
So something tells this blackened heart
  Of heavenly airs that blow
Where dwells the soul with God apart,
  And spotless lilies grow.

Yet still I find that murky street
  A fascinating lure,
I want to hear the tramp of feet
  And keep a spirit pure ;
O give me, God, the stainless white
  That lines the sea-bird's wing,
To keep the sooty Thames in sight
  And holy songs to sing !

A. W.—From the *Daily Chronicle.*

LIFE ! I KNOW NOT WHAT THOU ART.

LIFE ! I know not what thou art,
　　But know that thou and I must part ;
And when, or how, or where we met,
I own to me's a secret yet.

＊　　＊　　＊　　＊　　＊

Life ! we've been long together,
Through pleasant and through cloudy weather ;
'Tis hard to part when friends are dear ;
Perhaps 'twill cost a sigh, a tear ;
—Then steal away, give little warning,
Choose thine own time ;
Say not Good-night—but in some brighter clime
Bid me Good-Morning.

ANNA LETITIA BARBAULD.

Portions omitted.

IN THE HOUR OF DEATH.

IN the hour of death, after this life's whim,
  When the heart beats low, and the eyes grow dim,
And pain has exhausted every limb—
The lover of the Lord shall trust in Him.

When the will has forgotten the life-long aim,
And the mind can only disgrace its fame,
And a man is uncertain of his own name—
The power of the Lord shall fill this frame.

When the last sigh is heaved, and the last tear shed,
And the coffin is waiting beside the bed,
And the widow and child forsake the dead—
The angel of the Lord shall lift this head.

For even the purest delight may pall,
And power must fail, and the pride must fall,
And the love of the dearest friends grow small—
But the glory of the Lord is all in all.

R. D. BLACKMORE.

XI.
HYMNS

CHILD, AMID THE FLOWERS AT PLAY.

CHILD, amid the flowers at play,
　　While the red light fades away ;
Mother, with thine earnest eye,
Ever following silently ;
Father, by the breeze of eve
Called thy harvest work to leave—
Pray : ere yet the dark hours be,
Lift the heart and bend the knee !
Traveller, in the stranger's land,
Far from thine own household band ;
Mourner, haunted by the tone
Of a voice from this world gone ;
Captive, in whose narrow cell
Sunshine hath not leave to dwell ;
Sailor, on the darkening sea—
Lift the heart and bend the knee.

*　　*　　*　　*　　*

Ye that triumph, ye that sigh,
Kindred by one holy tie,
Heaven's first star alike ye see—
Lift the heart and bend the knee !

FELICIA HEMANS.

O PERFECT LOVE.

"The Lord do so to me and more also, if ought but death part thee and me."

O PERFECT Love, all human thought transcending,
  Lowly we kneel in prayer before Thy throne,
That theirs may be the love which knows no ending,
  Whom Thou for evermore dost join in one.

O perfect Life, be Thou their full assurance
  Of tender charity and steadfast faith,
Of patient hope, and quiet brave endurance,
  With childlike trust that fears nor pain nor death.

Grant them the joy which brightens earthly sorrow,
  Grant them the peace which calms all earthly strife ;
And to life's day the glorious unknown morrow
  That dawns upon eternal love and life.

MRS. GURNEY.

THERE'S A WIDENESS IN GOD'S MERCY.

THERE'S a wideness in God's mercy
    Like the wideness of the sea ;
There's a kindness in His justice,
    Which is more than liberty.

For the love of God is broader
    Than the measures of man's mind ;
And the Heart of the Eternal
    Is most wonderfully kind.

If our love were but more Simple,
    We should take Him at His word ;
And our lives would be all sunshine
    In the sweetness of our Lord.

F. W. FABER.

Verses omitted.

FIGHT THE GOOD FIGHT.

FIGHT the good fight with all thy might,
　　Christ is thy Strength, and Christ thy Right ;
Lay hold on life and it shall be
Thy joy and crown eternally.

Run the straight race through God's good grace,
Lift up thine eyes and seek His Face ;
Life with its way before us lies,
Christ is the path, and Christ the prize.

Cast care aside, lean on thy Guide ;
His boundless mercy will provide ;
Trust, and thy trusting soul shall prove
Christ is its life, and Christ its love.

Faint not nor fear, His Arms are near,
He changeth not, and thou art dear ;
Only believe, and thou shalt see
That Christ is all in all to thee.

J. S. B. MONSELL.

SWING LOW, SWEET CHARIOT.

SWING low, sweet chariot,
  Coming for to carry me home.
Swing low, sweet chariot,
Coming for to carry me home.

I looked over Jordan,
What did I see,
Coming for to carry me home?
A band of angels coming after me—
Coming for to carry me home.

Swing low, sweet chariot,
Coming for to carry me home.
Swing low, sweet chariot,
Coming for to carry me home.

A Negro Spiritual.

BATTLE HYMN OF THE AMERICAN REPUBLIC.

MINE eyes have seen the glory of the coming of the
Lord :
He is trampling out the vintage where the grapes of wrath
are stored ;
He hath loosed the fatal lightning of his terrible swift
sword :
       His truth is marching on.

I have seen Him in the watchfires of a hundred circling
camps ;
They have builded Him an altar in the evening dews and
damps ;
I can read His righteous sentence by the dim and flaring
lamps :
       His day is marching on.

I have read a fiery gospel writ in burnish'd rows of steel :
" As ye deal with my contemners, so with you my grace
shall deal ;
Let the Hero, born of woman, crush the serpent with His
heel !
       Since God is marching on."

He has sounded forth the trumpet that shall never call
retreat ;
He is sifting out the hearts of men before His judgment
seat ;
O, be swift, my soul to answer Him, be jubilant my feet !
       Our God is marching on.

In the beauty of the lilies Christ was born, across the sea,
With a glory in His bosom that transfigures you and me :
As He died to make men holy, let us live to make men free,
    While God is marching on.

JULIA WARD HOWE.

Made and Printed in Great Britain by C. TINLING & Co. LTD.,
53 Victoria Street, Liverpool, and at London and Prescot